CW01582712

Haddenham & Aldreth
Past and Present

Haddenham & Aldreth
Past and Present

a millennium celebration
in photographs old and new

Fern House

First published in 2000 by
Fern House
High Street Haddenham
Cambridgeshire CB6 3XA

www.fernhouse.com

© Copyright Haddenham Parish Council
and the contributors

Copyright enquiries should be addressed first to the publisher

A catalogue record for this book
is available from the British Library

ISBN 1 902702 06 9

Printed in England by TJ International Ltd, Padstow

Acknowledgements

A book such as this would not come into being without the help and co-operation of the large number of individuals and organisations who have supplied photographs, information, finance and support.

We are grateful to the following for their financial support:
East Cambridgeshire District Council
The Haddenham Charities
Haddenham Parish Council.

We are particularly grateful to Freda Crofts and Lorna Delanoy for their invaluable source material and memories.

Alphabetically, others who have contributed include:
Ann & Andy Biggs
The Cambridgeshire Collection
Judith Dale
David Fairchild
The Haddenham Charities
Haddenham Parish Council and its Millennium Working Party
Alastair Hull
Jenny Manning
The staff and pupils of the Robert Arkenstall Primary School
Robert Norman
Shirley Pollard
Sheila Searle.
Keith & Sheila West

Thanks to those at Fern House who helped to prepare the book:
Zoë Dale
Charlotte Edwards
Matt Pettitt
Chris Winch.

Much gratitude to all the above, and our profuse apologies for any errors in or omissions from the lists.

Rodney Dale

"THE ELMS", FROIZE END,
HADDENHAM, Ely, Cambs.

.... 194

M ....

Dr to. J. H. HANDLEY,

Greengrocer and Fruit Agent.

CARTAGE WORK CATERED FOR.

Telephone: STD (035 374) HADDENHAM 284 and 308 (Pig Dept.) V.A.T. Reg. No. 213 4765 77

J. HANDLEY & SONS

NURSERYMEN AND PIG FARMERS

J. M. Handley
P. Handley, B.Sc. (Hort.)
E. V. Handley
J. E. Handley

THE ELMS,
LODE WAY,
HADDENHAM,
CAMBS. CB6 3UL

Telephone: Ely 740308 & 740723 V.A.T. Reg. No. 213 4765 77

J. HANDLEY & SONS

NURSERYMEN AND PIG FARMERS

P. Handley, B.Sc. (Hort.)
J.E. Handley
M.P. Handley
S.J. Handley
D.W. Handley

THE ELMS,
LODE WAY,
HADDENHAM,
CAMBS. CB6 3UL

J. Handley & Sons

Year Round Chrysanthemum Growers

88A Aldreth Road
Haddenham
Cambs
CB6 3PN

Phone 01353 741480
Fax 01353 741480

Development of a family business

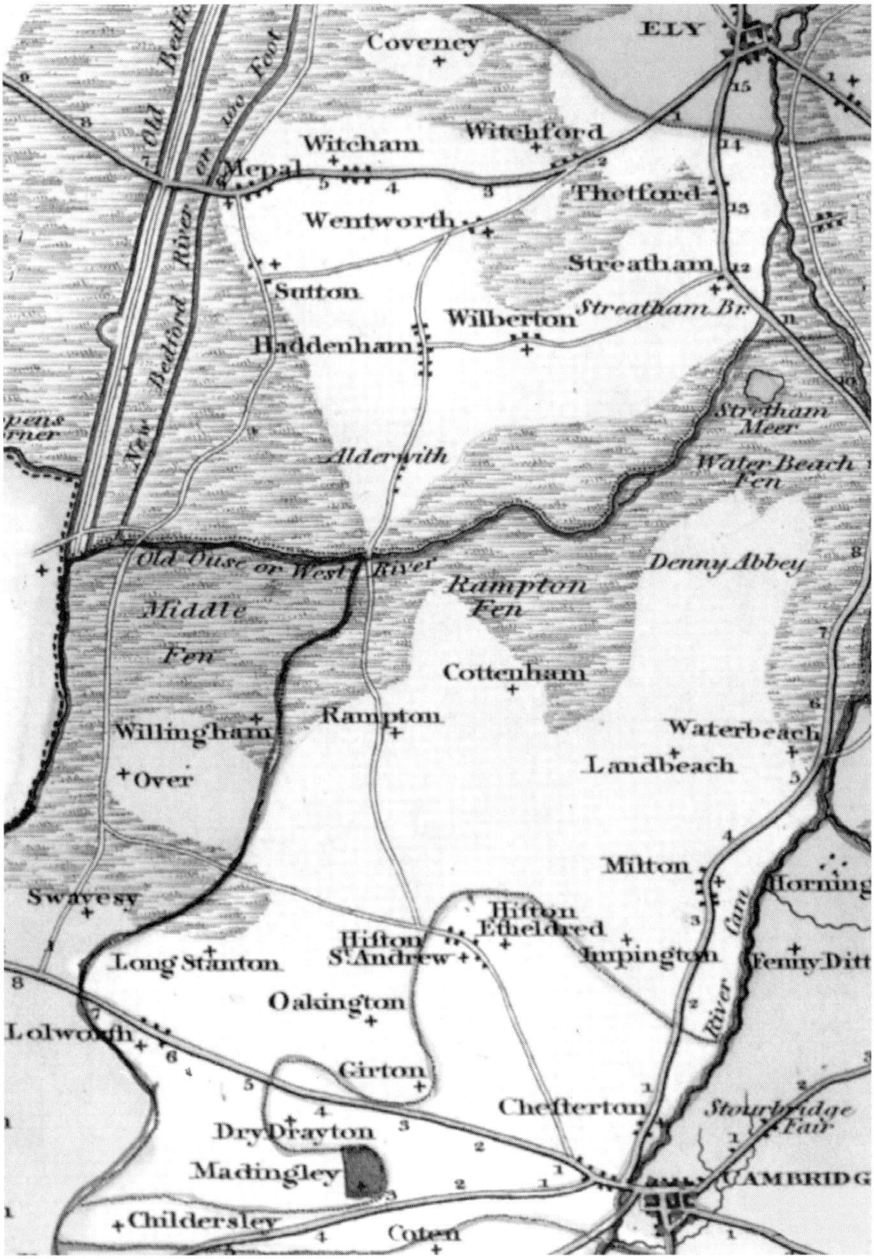

Thomas Dix's map of Cambridgeshire and the Isle of Ely published on 12 August 1816 shows the past arrangement of the roads linking Haddenham and the surrounding villages.

Introduction

Haddenham occupies high ground in the Cambridgeshire Fens about 14 miles north of Cambridge and seven miles south-west of Ely.

The 'new millennium' is doubly significant to Haddenham; we are celebrating not only 2,000 years of the Christian Era, but also 1,000 years of Haddenham. The earliest mention of the name of the parish is found in a Saxon record of 970AD, which refers to Hæden Ham or Haeda's Homestead.

In the Domesday Book (1086) the parish is divided into three manors: Hadreham, Helle (now Hillrow) and Lindone (now Linden End). At about the same time, there is mention of Aldery (now Aldreth), Haddenham's southerly companion hamlet.

The settlement of Haddenham no doubt came into being because of the presence of the ridge on which it stands. There is much evidence of early occupancy of the area, and the Neolithic burial chamber discovered in 1987 is about 6,000 years old, one of the oldest in Europe. The discovery of the Saxon grave on the crest of the ridge (now in the car park of The Three Kings) prompts one to close one's eyes and and imagine what it must have been like to stand there all that time ago, looking over the flat, reedy fenland landscape to the north and the south. On a clear day, the north panorama takes in the cathedrals at Peterborough and Ely; to the south is what was one of the main roads into the village, the direction from which Hereward the Wake is reputed to have marched to make his last stand against the Normans at Aldreth.

The east–west ridge is now marked by the line of the A1123, from Huntingdon, St Ives and Earith to the west, passing through Haddenham to Wilburton, Stretham and Soham to the east. Haddenham now stands at a crossroads, with Station Road sloping down to the north and the High Street sloping down to the south and thence to Aldreth. From whichever direction you approach Haddenham, you have to go up a hill.

Hod Hall Lane, HADDENHAM, Cambs.

195

M R A Freeman

BOUGHT OF

S. A. BURGESS

Motor and Agricultural Engineer

INVOICE

Nº 1798

J. W. RICHARDS

Haulage Contractor

HADDENHAM · CAMBS

Telephones: HADDENHAM 397 and 438

DAILY SERVICE TO DERBY BIRMINGHAM MANSFIELD NOTTINGHAM LEICESTER COVENTRY

LOADS UP TO 16 TONS DROPSIDES FLATS TIPPERS ALWAYS AVAILABLE

M H.R.Freeman Esq.,

High Street, Haddenham, Ely, Cambs.

February 5th 1968

Brought forward from other page......

15th 306573 11T. 7C.0Q. Beet to Ely.

306706 10T. 0C.0Q.

22&T.12C.0Q. Beet to Ely @ 10/6d P.T. £118 19 4 d.

Plus 1/- P.T. Loading...... 11 6 7

£130 5 11d.

Telephone: Haddenham 289

Bought of C. F. BESTER

Seedsman and Horticultural Sundries

Agent for Plant Protection Products

HIGH STREET, HADDENHAM, Cambs.

M A. Freeman 25th March 1957

HADDENHAM, ISLE OF ELY

195

M H Freeman

DR. TO

SYDNEY FEAST

Builder and Contractor

Agent to the London and Lancashire Fire Insurance Company

M A Freeman

Feb 21 1949

ROLAND ALSOP,

GROCER & DRAPER,

HADDENHAM, ELY, CAMBS.

Agent for Bee's & Ryder's Seeds. All Farm Seeds.

Dealer in Skins and Feathers Rabbits for killing.

Some Haddenham billheads of the past.

This book comprises a commentary and photographs taking you on a walk round the parish. We have in many places contrasted the old with the new ('new' being 1999) but you must remember that what is new now will in due course become old, and thus of even greater interest to future generations than it is now.

We will start our walk at the crossroads, at the Top Shop (Top Corner), go down the east side of the road to Aldreth, and back up the west side of the road to the crossroads (Gooby's Corner). We will then go west down The Green, West End and Hillrow, back to the crossroads (Sun Dial Corner), down Station Road and back (Windmill Corner), then to Hop Row and out towards Wilburton and back to Top Corner.

On our way we will look at local activities and events past and present – brick making, farming, the floods, flower and fruit growing, milling, the railway and so on.

Every child of school age in the village is to receive a copy of the book, so we include pictures of each class in the School, with names. We also include a record of the members of the Parish Council, and the Trustees of the local Charities.

Notwithstanding the sterling work of Freda Crofts who has amassed a photographic archive envied by other parishes, there are still gaps in the record. Many people have unearthed further material during the preparation of this book, and we are grateful to them for allowing us to make an electronic record of their pictures. We have not been able to use them all in the book, but we have added them to the local collection in the library.

If anyone else has pictures and other material showing how we lived then – or how we live now – we would be pleased to add it to the electronic archive for posterity.

Rodney Dale

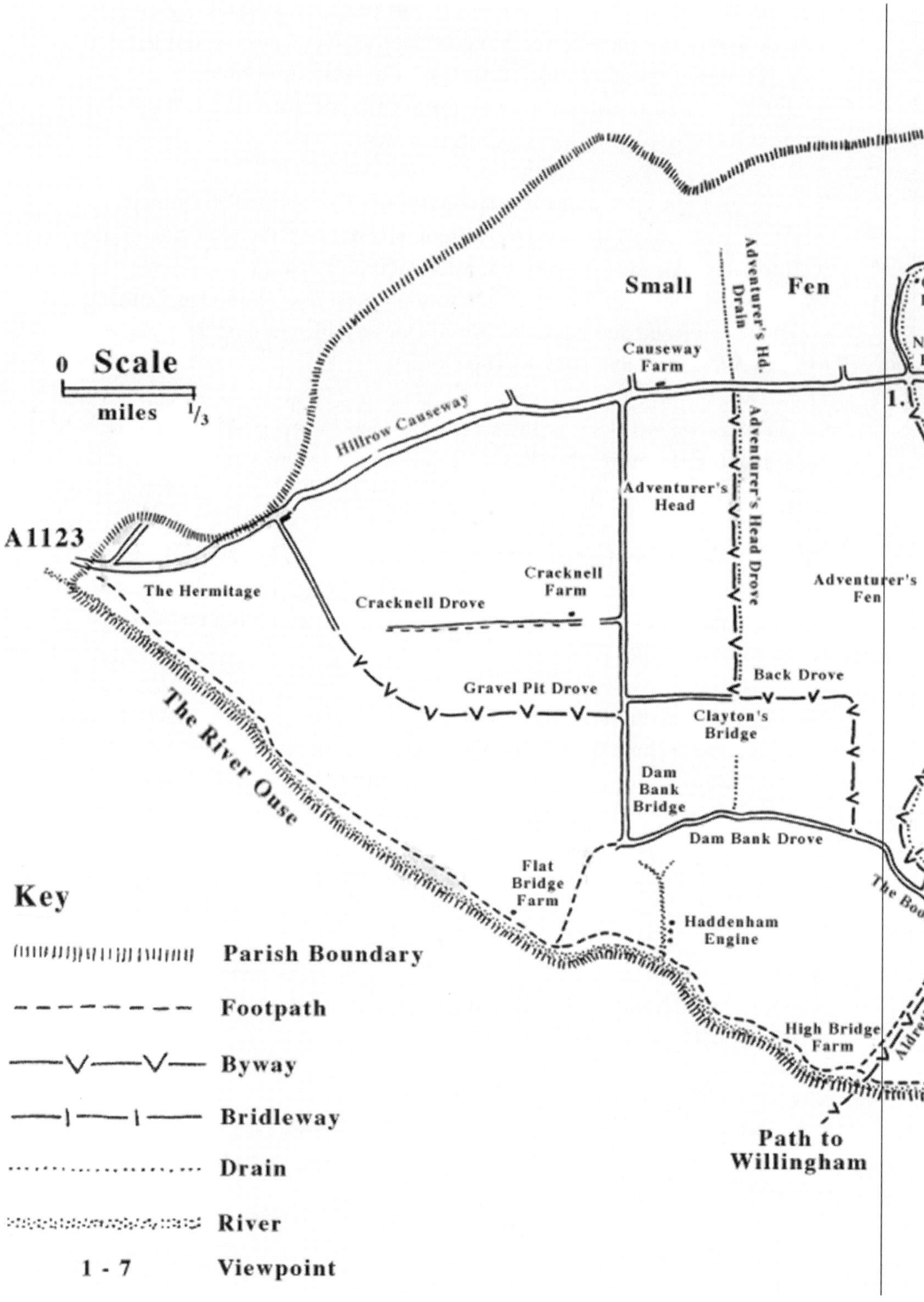
Small
Fen
Adventurer's Hd. Drain
Causeway Farm
0 Scale
miles 1/3
Hillrow Causeway
Adventurer's Head
Adventurer's Head Drove
A1123
The Hermitage
Cracknell Drove
Cracknell Farm
Adventurer's Fen
Back Drove
Gravel Pit Drove
Clayton's Bridge
The River Ouse
Dam Bank Bridge
Dam Bank Drove
Flat Bridge Farm
Haddenham Engine
High Bridge Farm
Path to Willingham
Key
Parish Boundary
Footpath
Byway
Bridleway
Drain
River
1 - 7
Viewpoint

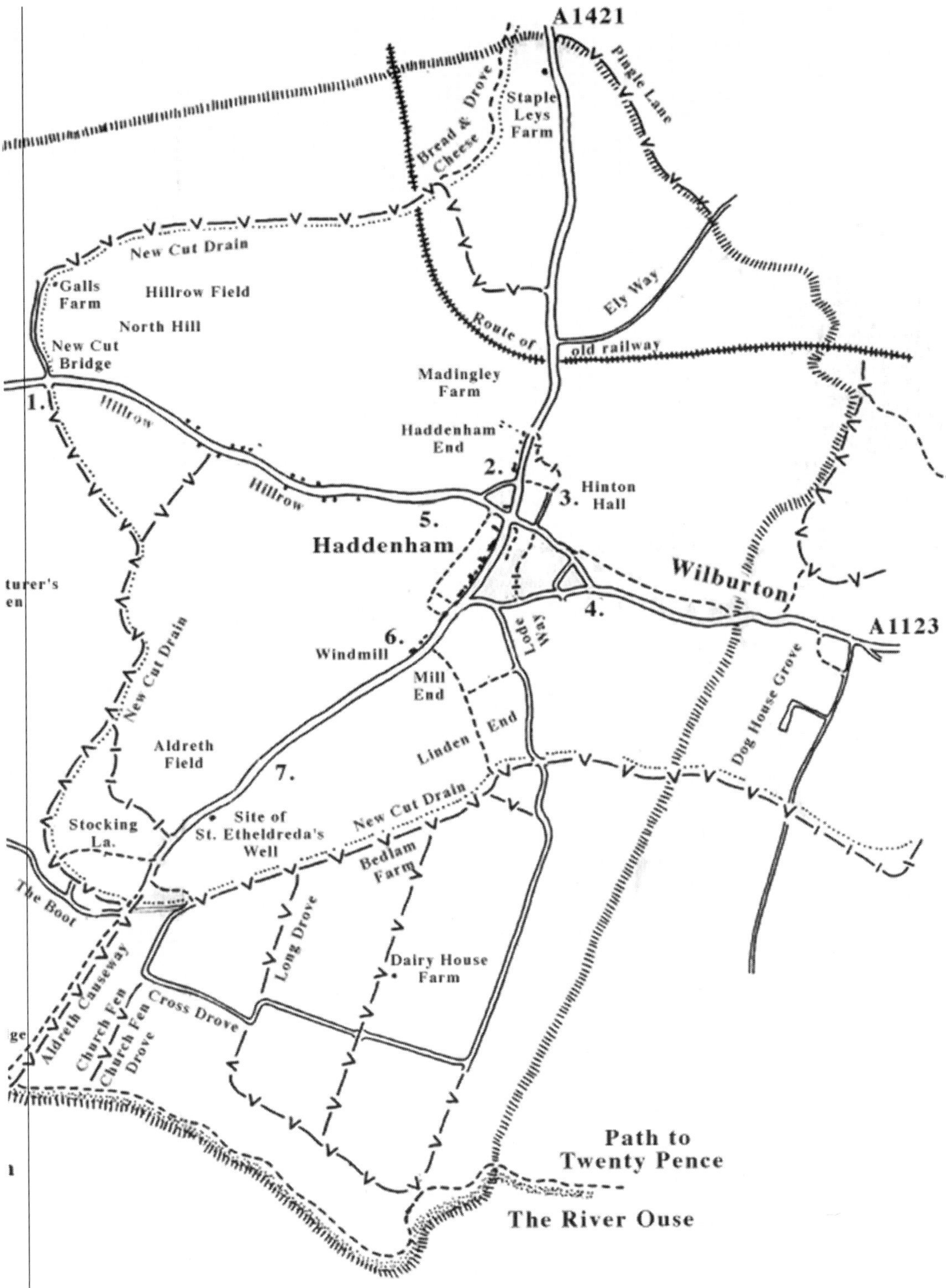
A1421
Pingle Lane
Staple Leys Farm
Bread & Cheese Drove
New Cut Drain
Galls Farm
Hillrow Field
North Hill
New Cut Bridge
Ely Way
Route of old railway
Madingley Farm
Haddenham End
1.
Hillrow
Hillrow
2.
3.
Hinton Hall
5.
Haddenham
Wilburton
4.
A1123
6.
Windmill
Lode Way
Mill End
Linden End
Dog House Grove
New Cut Drain
Aldreth Field
7.
Stocking La.
Site of St. Etheldreda's Well
New Cut Drain
Bedlam Farm
The Boot
Long Drove
Dairy House Farm
Aldreth Causeway
Church Fen
Church Fen Drove
Cross Drove
Path to Twenty Pence
The River Ouse

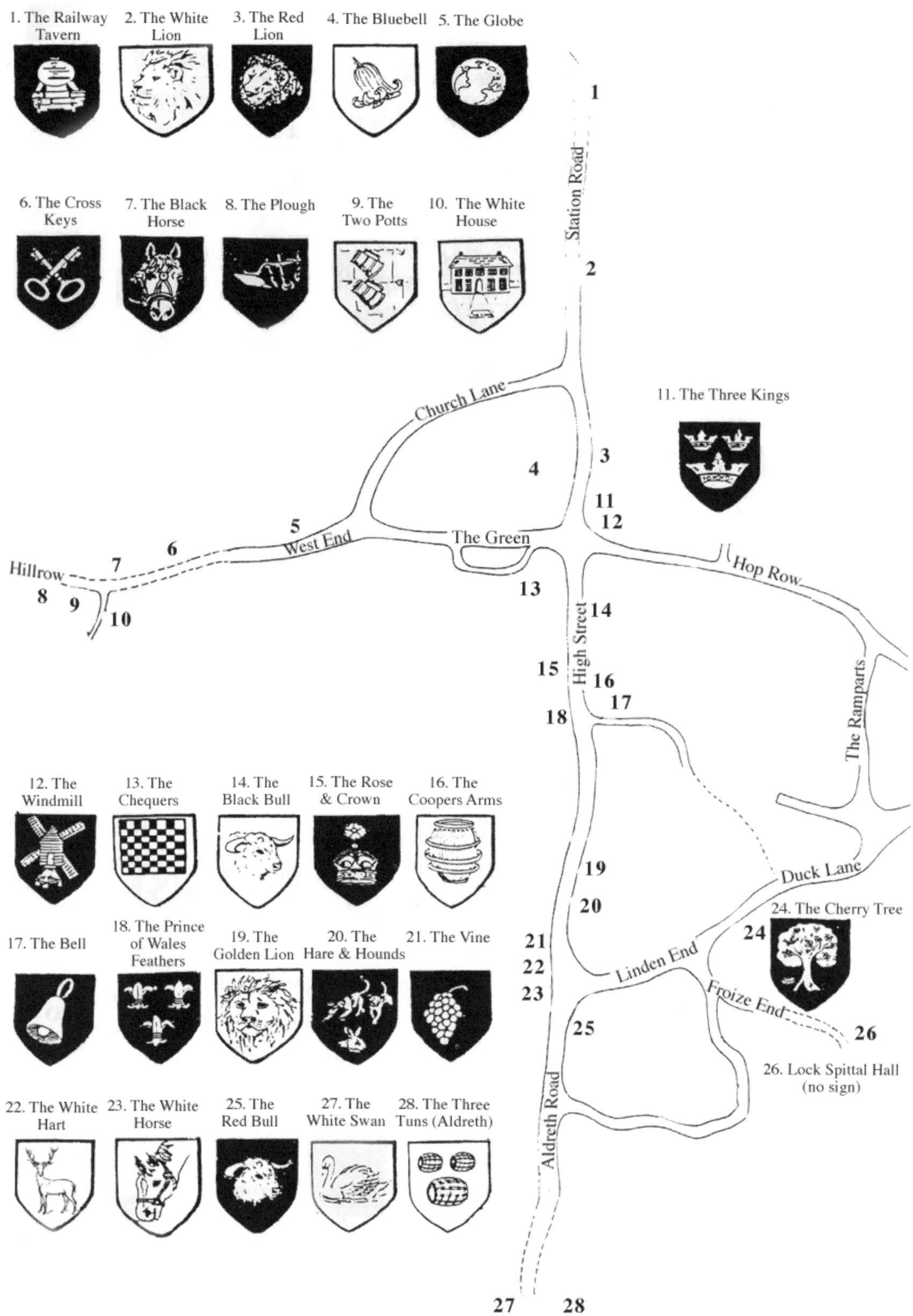
1. The Railway Tavern
2. The White Lion
3. The Red Lion
4. The Bluebell
5. The Globe
6. The Cross Keys
7. The Black Horse
8. The Plough
9. The Two Potts
10. The White House
11. The Three Kings
12. The Windmill
13. The Chequers
14. The Black Bull
15. The Rose & Crown
16. The Coopers Arms
17. The Bell
18. The Prince of Wales Feathers
19. The Golden Lion
20. The Hare & Hounds
21. The Vine
22. The White Hart
23. The White Horse
24. The Cherry Tree
25. The Red Bull
26. Lock Spittal Hall (no sign)
27. The White Swan
28. The Three Tuns (Aldreth)
Station Road
Church Lane
West End
The Green
Hillrow
Hop Row
High Street
The Ramparts
Duck Lane
Linden End
Froize End
Aldreth Road
1
2
3
4
5
6
7
8
9
10
11
12
13
14
15
16
17
18
19
20
21
22
23
24
25
26
27
28

Public houses in the past were very different from what they are today. In those days people brewed beer in their homes and sold it to a very local clientele. The fact that there were nearly 30 public houses in the village a century ago reflects this practice. The importance here is that, on our walk round the village, we will be passing many of the sites where public houses used to stand, and this will form part of our story.

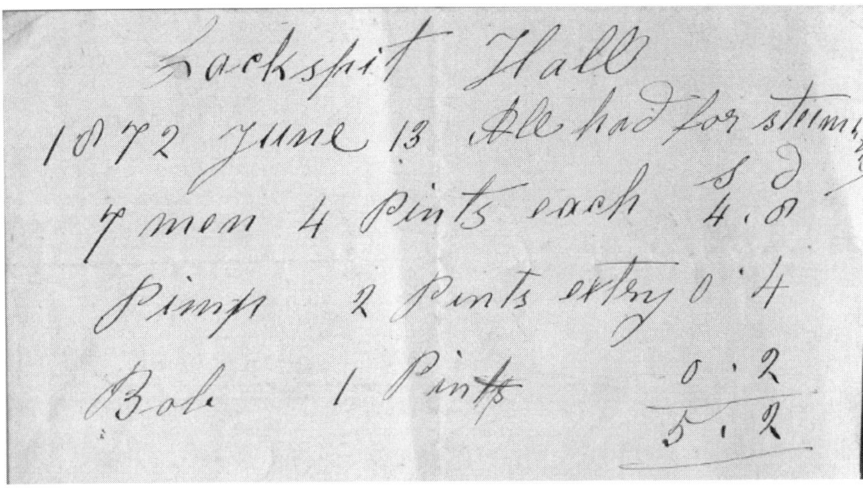
Lockspit Hall
1872 June 13 Ale had for steaming
7 men 4 Pints each s d 4.8
Pimps 2 Pints extry 0.4
Bole 1 Pints 0.2
5.2

An early ephemeral item – a receipt for 'Ale had for steaming' at tuppence (0.8p) a pint, from Lockspit(al) Hall dated 13 June 1872. Below is a billhead three years older putting 'steaming' into context.

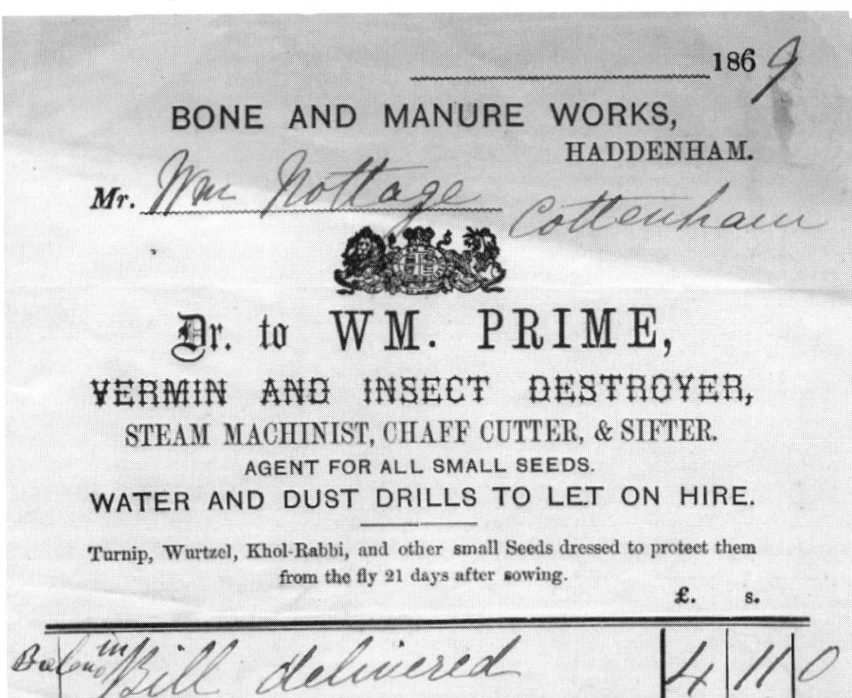
1869
BONE AND MANURE WORKS,
HADDENHAM.
Mr. Wm Nottage Cottenham
Dr. to WM. PRIME,
VERMIN AND INSECT DESTROYER,
STEAM MACHINIST, CHAFF CUTTER, & SIFTER.
AGENT FOR ALL SMALL SEEDS.
WATER AND DUST DRILLS TO LET ON HIRE.
Turnip, Wurtzel, Khol-Rabbi, and other small Seeds dressed to protect them from the fly 21 days after sowing.
£. s.
Bill delivered 4 11 0

Tebbutt's Shop known as the 'Top Shop', standing as it does at Top Corner. Mr Tebbutt was a well-known figure in the local community; his daughter Jessie followed in his footsteps, and it was through her efforts that we now have a library in the village, and her idea that the redundant Arkenstall Boys' School could be turned into a village centre.

Today, the Top Shop is run by Dillons. The lower part of the building is much the same, but the chimney stacks and dormer windows have gone. The house beyond has a mansard roof – a feature of many houses in Haddenham.

Originally the Black Bull Inn (14), this was the home of Dr Kinder who died in 1893 aged 43 leaving four young sons. Dr Howe also lived here. The house with the steps was occupied by Adam Palmer the watchmaker, and next to this is Mr Sid Carter's General Stores which moved here after his shop was burnt down with others that stood along the front of what is now the Arkenstall Car Park. The further house in the picture became the Co-operative Stores, with large shop windows. The Doctor's house became the newsagent and Mr Carter's was demolished to make way for a bungalow.

Inset: Still visible is the mouthpiece of Doctor Kinder's speaking tube mounted in the left hand door post, so that people could consult him at night.

The Doctor's house today; its chimney stacks – like so many others in the village – have been truncated, and the further side of its frontage now has another door and a shop window. Beyond it is the bungalow that replaced Mr Carter's shop, and then the building that became the Co-op.

The front of Walkers newsagent and general store occupying the right-hand side of the Doctor's house.

The Co-op Stores as it stood empty for quite a few years until it was …

… restored to its former glory as private houses.

A model of the refurbished Co-op with other new buildings on the site.

Looking up the High Street with No 15 in the foreground.

Another view of the elaborate front of No 15; Palmer's butchers beyond.

No 15 as it is today, a private house. The brickwork clearly shows the modifications to the windows.

Arthur 'Porky' Palmer's Pork Butcher's Shop at 17 High Street, to the left of Fern House (No 19). It became Victors, Mr 'Chemmy' Steel's ironmonger's shop, when he left the premises in what had been The Windmill on top corner.

Victors Hardware – Mr Steel's shop which replaced Palmer's butchers shop in the 1930s. The premises became an estate agent's office and is now Hereward Books, specialising in hunting, shooting and fishing.

Inset: Doug and Cecily Steel, last owners of Victors Hardware, before they retired in 1993.

The Post Office (No 21) as it is today. Earlier, it was Alf Drake's ironmonger's and bicycle repair shop, and the Post Office was in a house opposite

These old cottages with date stone 1742 were demolished to make way for the road into Camping Close and the new Robert Arkenstall Primary School. The white building was The Bell (17), whose last landlord was Henry Hawes.

Another view of the demolished cottages; wheelwright Harry Savage looks over the wall.

The corner where the houses were removed to make way for Camping Close and the new School. The walnut tree on the green bank used to stand in Jack Cockle's garden; before the Second World War he planted a seedling he found in Hillrow Fen where he worked for E J Burton. As recorded on the plaque, Jack was awarded the Military Medal in World War II.

The Robert Arkenstall Primary School, Camping Close. The building on the left is the school hall; to the right is the staff common room.

Sheltered housing in Camping Close.

Late 18th-century house, with original top windows, which was probably turned into a shop in the 19th century. At the turn of the 20th century it belonged to a Mr Collins; it was taken over in 1933 by ED Crofts, who is standing in the doorway. The cottage with a mansard roof beyond it is a listed is a listed building.

When the Crofts family retired, the premises became first a fish and chip shop; then a Chinese take away. The far end became a cycle, CB and video shop but the whole property has now reverted to a private house. Note the fire-insurance sign above the door.

Stone Cross Farm, earlier a Quaker meeting house; names still survive on the barn wall to the left of the photo. Later it was a free house known as The Red Bull (25). It was bought by William Freeman in 1915, destroyed by lightning in 1923 and rebuilt to a traditional farmhouse design. It is now occupied by William Freeman's grandson Robert.

Stone Cross Farm (left) and Linden House (right), November 1999.

Linden End – a Horse waits to be shoed outside Miller's the Blacksmith's shop at Stone Cross Corner. The listed barn at the end of the building on the right is now a store. The houses to right and left of the smithy were The White Hart (22) and – appropriately enough – The White Horse (23).

The Cherry Tree (24), one of the two remaining public houses in the village, stands in an area renowned for its fruit growing – the Cherry Orchard Estate was built on a Cherry Orchard.

The Elms, Lode Way, was a large, thatched red-brick house: its farmyard is now Metcalfe Way (see below) and its orchard opposite – complete with Dovehouse – was developed for housing in the 1990s.

Some local building traditions are remembered in Metcalfe Way.

Looking up Lode Way from the corner of Nelson's Lane (October 1999).

Orchards were very much a part of the landscape in the south-east quarter of the village. When the railway arrived in the 1860s, it gave growers access to a wider market. Apple, pear and plum orchards stretched from Haddenham to Wilburton and down to Aldreth. The fruit season started in the spring with gooseberries and strawberries, and on to plums and apples, providing work for many of the local women. After the war lorries began to take over from the railways running a daily service to London and markets in the Midlands.

A group of apple pickers in the Aldreth Road Orchard in the 1960s having their 'dockey' or 'onesies'.

Left to right: Tom Hitch, Violet Barnes, Betty Stringer, Jeremy Norman, Blanche Smith, Gladys Holden, Nellie Thaxter, Robert Norman and Ivy Wakefield at Robert Norman's Orchard in Aldreth Road.

Strawberry pickers on Chivers Farm in Aldreth. The fruit was sent to the Chivers jam factory in Histon. The Chivers family were staunch Baptists, and gave generously for the Baptist Chapels in both Aldreth and Haddenham..

Arthur Markwell, at one time one of at least half-a-dozen chrysanthemum growers in the village. Gary Bethell, Peter Handley and Janet Markwell continue the tradition.

Peter Handley's high-tech chrysanthemum nursery.

Looking towards Aldreth; on the left the Great Mill built in 1803, and restored nearly 200 years later. Neville's Mill is behind the house on the right.

(Right) A rare view of Neville's Mill, long since demolished – locals said 'there weren't enough wind for the two on 'em.'

These were tower mills; the fantail turns the cap so that the sails face into the wind. This early example of a servo mechanism was patented in 1745.

Neville's Mill had a vertical fantail frame. The Great Mill had a sloping frame – as it has today – an unusual design for Cambridgeshire.

The Great Mill standing derelict after it stopped working in 1946. Fortunately the last Miller, John Lawrance, forbade anyone to remove any of the workings, so though the fabric gradually deteriorated, the parts were available for restoration or copying.

In 1992, the Law family moved into the Mill House, and employed the millwrights R. Thompson & Sons, who had looked after the Mill in years gone by, to restore it, with grants from East Cambs DC, the Heritage Lottery Fund, and the Pilgrim Trust.

Below left: the framework of the new cap and fantail assembly on the ground before it was lifted into position in December 1994.
Below right: the fourth sail frame about to be attached to its stock the following year.
The cap is 18 feet in diameter, and the sail stocks 36 ft long.

Looking down Aldreth Road from the Haddenham direction. The panorama of Aldreth stretches away to the left, and beyond lies Holme Fen, the River Ouse (or Old West), Smithey Fen and Cottenham.

The Baptist Chapels at both Aldreth and Haddenham received considerable finance from the Chivers family who owned a lot of land at Aldreth and had several 'tied' cottages there. In Aldreth, the land was given by the Prime family, and the finance by the Chivers family. Worship ceased at Aldreth in the late 1990s and the property offered for sale. For several years the building was used by the Tinderbox Playgroup.

For the next century – Nine Acre Wood stands at the very south of the parish boundary (OS Grid Reference TL 444 723). It was planted by volunteers in 1995 with four varieties of poplar and a mixture of a dozen other native broad leaved trees. It has been designed to attract the rare golden oriole, a yellow bird the size of a thrush which sings evocatively from the tree tops.

The southern boundary of the Parish – the Great Ouse or Old West River – as it passes Nine-acre Wood.

Looking down Aldreth High Street towards the Causeway and High Bridge. This area is traditionally thought to be the site of Hereward the Wake's battle with the Norman invaders towards the end of the 11th Century.

The east-facing gables remain the same, but the north-facing ones have been rebuilt to a less-interesting style.

These cottages form an attractive feature in the High Street at Aldreth: note mansard roof and red telephone box.

This house has been modernised and extended but the central inscription remains: '1906 G&CC'. It was once part of the assets of Gonville & Caius College; Cambridge colleges owned much land in the parish – for example, Petrus Field was owned by Peterhouse until bought by the Freeman family in 1917.

A view to the West End ridge showing Newtown, an estate built by the old Ely Rural District Council just after the First World War.

This row of refurbished cottages was given the name 'Winston' by its owners, the Jacksons. Could this be a tribute to the Great British Bulldog of the Second World War?

New and old – (*above*) the charm of village infill (completed 1998); (*below*) these cottages were the home of Albert Thulborn, Haddenham's last mole catcher. The art of staying in business as a mole catcher is to make sure that some are left to breed for the next season.

The White Hart (22), the home of well-known village character Naomi Jackson *ca* 1950.

House standing on the site of The White Hart.

Liverpool House, Mr Peters's general store. The Peters family owned the Great Mill from 1901 to 1906. This shop closed at the beginning of the Second World War.

Liverpool House, October 1999. The old shop window remains as a focal point for village posters. The bungalow on the right stands on the site of The Vine (21)

Part of the dairy display at the Farmland Museum when it was in the High Street. The Museum began as a child's collection in 1969; the artefacts grew to occupy a one-acre site. Money was raised for a variety of children's charities. The Museum closed in 1992 and is now rehoused as part of the Cambridgeshire agricultural collection at Denny Abbey on the A10. In 1998, Mike and Lorna Delanoy were each awarded an MBE for their part in preserving Fenland agricultural history.

This property in course of restoration dates from Georgian times, and was at one time the local newsagent's. The small side extension was used by Harry Collin the local tailor.

Rear view of property once on the site now occupied by Feast Lodge (below). The flower garden featured a summer house made from an early automobile.

Feast Lodge is solidly built in the Feast family tradition. The Feasts were responsible for many houses and public buildings in the area.

Looking up the High Street. In the present-day view (*below*) No 32 (left) with its ornate brickwork has been painted, and the houses beyond rebuilt. The spire of the Baptist Church is visible on the horizon. It is clear which of the houses on the right have been demolished to make way for Camping Close.

Mr Charles Bester's cottage at 26 High Street. He moved to Haddenham with his wife Elsie in 1934, and set up as a seedsman and horticultural supplier. Charles Bester was a Parish Councillor from 1937 to 1942; then Clerk to the Parish Council until 1983.

The rebuilt No 26 High Street.

The School for girls and mixed infants opened in 1861, and closed in 1970. It was the home of Spaceward Microsystems for a few years, before it was converted into five dwellings in the late 1990s.

A feature of the school buildings is the ornate brickwork, seen on the gable ends (above) and the bell tower and rose window (below).

Group 1 *Back Row*: Frank Peters, A Markham, Henry Howard, C Green, Sid Metcalfe, Ruby Searle –, Robert Sulman, Ruth Emery, Margaret Marwell *Middle Row*: –, George Newell, Win Lant, George Croxon, Victor Wright, Alice Burton, –, Hilda Jackson, Connie Pettingell *Front Row*: G Markwell, Cyril Gothard, Beattie Green, – Howard, –, Flossie Alsop, Henry Gotobed, Clifford Powers, G Bearcock, Ivy Gothard

Group 2 *Back Row*: Miss Howard, E Metcalfe, V Holden, G Amory, S Amory, Peter B Green, –, –, –, Miss Chambers *Middle Row*: T Green, Ada Metcalfe, H Patterson, – Howard, J Jackson, A Burgess, W Hill (?)
Front Row: E Burgess, A Holden, A Ransome, –, H Jackson, W Feast, A Feast.

Margaret Markwell (Group 1) who married Alf Ransome (Group 2) recalled the names 70 years after these pictures were taken.

This is the old Rose & Crown (15) which was taken over by Wright's the Bakers, who moved from higher up the street. When the last bakery in Haddenham closed in 1990, the premises became a fish and chip shop and later a Chinese take away as well.

Wright's bakery is now Alastair Hull's warehouse, art gallery and studios. Kilim expert Alastair travels central Asia, seeking the decorative and unusual.

Haddenham once had several bakeries. This was originally A Setchell's Shop, here occupied by Sykes, and then by Mallyons and Wrights. School children could buy two bread rolls for a penny in the 1940s.

When The Rose & Crown closed, Wrights moved their shop there and built a new bakehouse behind the premises. The shop front was reconstructed as it its today, occupied by the butchers Hills, Harnwell & Rutterford.

HIGH ST, SUTTON, ELY (01353) 778164
14 HIGH ST, HADDENHAM, ELY (01353) 740908

M...

Bot. of **HILLS, HARNWELL & RUTTERFORD**

Butchers

lbs.	ozs.	Net Weight as sold	@	£	p

As in many villages, non-conformity is strong in Haddenham. The Methodist (previously Wesleyan) Chapel is pictured before 1940, when the iron railings were collected for the War Effort – which turned out to be a futile gesture.

The building was completed in 1891 on the site of an earlier Wesleyan Chapel and to its left is the baker's shop.

This House, now divided into flats, was once the home of the Village Library and Co-op Hardware Shop where Ellen Peters served as assistant for many years.

Looking at Gooby's Corner and down the High Street from the cross roads before 1920, when Haddenham had its own PC complete with bicycle, and you could stand and chat in the middle of the road. The Green is to the right.

Looking along The Green and down West End. Behind the finger-post stands a gipsy caravan.

Another view of Gooby's Corner.

Crossways Flats replaced the row of cottages on the corner by the Green in the early 1990s. The line of the Green is the same as in the previous picture, but the direction signs has become more obtrusive. The War Memorial has appeared on the right.

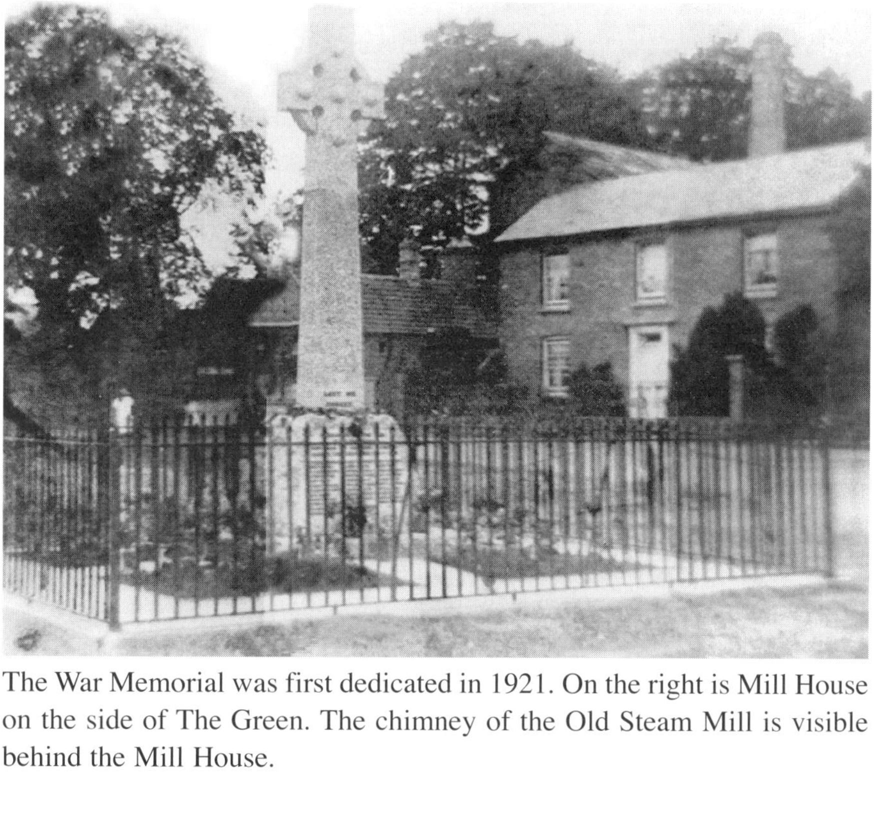

The War Memorial was first dedicated in 1921. On the right is Mill House on the side of The Green. The chimney of the Old Steam Mill is visible behind the Mill House.

Haddenham Feast on the Green, Hospital Sunday, held each year on Trinity Sunday. It was one of the highlights of the year, when families would gather – especially on the Sunday evening when the band played.

The Feast looking east. The spire of the Baptist Chapel stands out; in the distance to the right is Windmill Corner. The single-storey building on the extreme left is the old Fire-engine House. Not wanting to pay dues to Ely, Haddenham maintained its own fire brigade until it was called on to attend a straw fire down Station Road – then the hoses were found to be perished and the Ely Brigade had to be called after all.

View across the green with part of what was The Chequers on the left (13). To the right of The Chequers is Lloyd's Bank. The village has been without a bank since 1990. The house to the right of the bank belonged to the Feast family, well-known builders, who were responsible for the Methodist and Baptist Chapels, the Robert Arkenstall School, and many others local Buildings. The old Baptist Chapel is just visible on the far right.

The Haddenham sign was designed and built locally, and paid for by the Friends of Haddenham.

The Old Baptist Chapel was replaced by the present building on Sun Dial Corner in the 1900s. It was used for Evening Institute and School dinners, Badminton Club and Band Practice Room until being pulled down in late 1980s to make way for the modern Doctors' Surgery. Human remains from the graveyard at the front were reburied in the Parish Cemetery. Some of the coffins, it is said, were found to contain coal.

The new Doctors' Surgery, completed in the 1990s. The Haddenham Equipment and Resuscitation Trust (HEART) raises money to improve the facilities available. Note the boundary wall, skilfully renovated by Watts the builder; Haddenham has many attactive walls, both in the old red brick and the more modern white.

Newtown was a development of semi-detached houses built after the First World War.

The Newtown Pocket Park, opened Saturday 18 September 1999.

The floods of 1947

Flooding at Earith Bridge

The worst-ever flood disater since the fens were drained is still widely recalled. A combination of impermeably frozen soil, heavy snow and rain, and high winds, caused banks to burst and thousands of acres to become inundated. When it was clear that this would happen, people and livestock moved to higher ground, many to the aerodromes at Mepal and Witchford.

No crops grew in 1947; drilling was not possible until the spring of the following year. The floods were a salutary disaster, but out of them came revised drainage – and many other improvements – so that 'nothing like this can ever happen again'.

In his eye-witness account, local historian Charles Bester wrote: 'Straw stacks and farm buildings floated by like boats, and the waves were awash with floating potatoes, mangolds, and farm débris.'

We have to thank local amateur photographer Walter Martin Lane (second from the right) for his record of many of the dramatic scenes of floods and their effects.

The devastation caused by the force of the waters: 'Captain Flood will win in the end' is an old Fen saying.

Until this century, the majority of people living in the village depended on the land for their living. Agricultural wages were low, so women and children would work in the fields especially at harvest time and took on other seasonal work such as potato picking. Even when school attendance became compulsory, the absentee rate rose at certain times of the year.

Before the Second World War, there was a lot of hand work in farming. William Freeman and helpers riddling potatoes at Land's End Farm (now demolished) just beyond the Peterhouse field in Holme Fen.

Harvest work in the field behind the Black Horse Public House (7) Hillrow. The lady standing on the left is the landlady, Mrs Leopold Oakey, with Ethel Pake sitting in front. The man sitting on the right is Henry T Burton, a well-known local name.

Potato pickers' dockey break was taken about eleven o'clock at Hamence's Farm, Hillrow. Potatoes were no longer being picked up by hand when this was taken – a potato harvester was used. Farms were becoming mechanised.

Dovecotes, housing as many as 6,000 birds, were first built in about 1150. The birds were bred to be eaten; this was very economical, as they needed feeding only in the winter when there was snow on the ground and they could not forage for themselves.

Until the Middle Ages, doves were used for medicines; their blood was believed to cure bloodshot eyes, and a live bird cut in half and applied to the head would cure 'melancholy sadness'. The stomach lining, dried and powdered, was used for 'dysenteries'; the dung mixed with watercress for curing baldness and gout. The down and feathers filled pillows and feather beds, and it was said that if you slept on pigeon feathers you would live to a ripe old age.

Dovecotes, at one time a common sight, have now all but disappeared from the countryside. The last two in Haddenham were at Woolden Farm (*above*) and at Freeman's Farm in the High Street.

J Newell, Billy Newell, and G 'Wooler' Amory, with a corn stack ready for thatching in Hillrow. Threshing would take place at harvest time but also later in the year straight from the stack, which provided a form of storage.

Ploughing with two heavy horses. Each November horse teams, as well as tractors, compete in the Ploughing Match at Hermitage Farm. Competitors come from as far afield as Cornwall.

At the Haddenham & District Young Farmers' Club Ploughing Match, Saturday 2 November 1946. The champion team is on the left with Freddie Mitchell; the reserve champions on the right with Jack Burton. The photo (property of the YFC) is by Starr & Rignall, a well-known local firm.

George Pake ('Pakey') on a traction engine – note the belt drive round the flywheel going off to the left. Traction engines were used for powering all sorts of stationary farm machinery. The steam threshing tackle was a familiar sight up to the third decade of this century in Haddenham, and associated particularly with the names of Burkitt and Peacock. The story goes that William Burkitt never did his laces up after a red-hot coal fell into his boot.

Fowler's improved self-moving compound ploughing engine (about 1865). The cable which pulls the plough across the field is wound on a drum beneath the engine. The engine then moved forward a little, and the plough was reversed and pulled back. Either the engines were used in pairs, one on either side of the field, or a pulley was anchored on the other side so that one engine could pull the plough in either direction. There was great excitement when Chivers brought in steam tackle to plough the fields.

Before the war, Hillrow had its own shop run by Miss Russell.

The Porch House in Hillrow (or, as the postcard has it, Old Porched House, Hillnow) is regarded as one of the best domestic properties in the Parish. The porch bears the date 1657, but this may refer to the porch itself, rather than the whole building, parts of which are older. After falling into disrepair, the house was greatly restored in the 1960s and is now a family home.

There are several large former farmhouses along Hillrow; two are featured on this page. The Limes, with its attractive front porch (refurbished in 1999) and iron railings was once the home of Farmer Dennis, whose family still farms along the Earith Causeway.

Hill Row House was for many years the headquarters of Palmers the dairy people.

Globe House, formerly The Globe (5), stands at right angles to West End. Locals always called it The Sand Hole, because of the pit behind it in Church Lane.

The Old Steam Mill (see page 45), is now a private house. It was built in about 1850, and the construction is reminiscent of the steam-engine house at Stretham (built in 1831). The Mill was owned by Setchells and stopped working at the beginning of the Second World War.

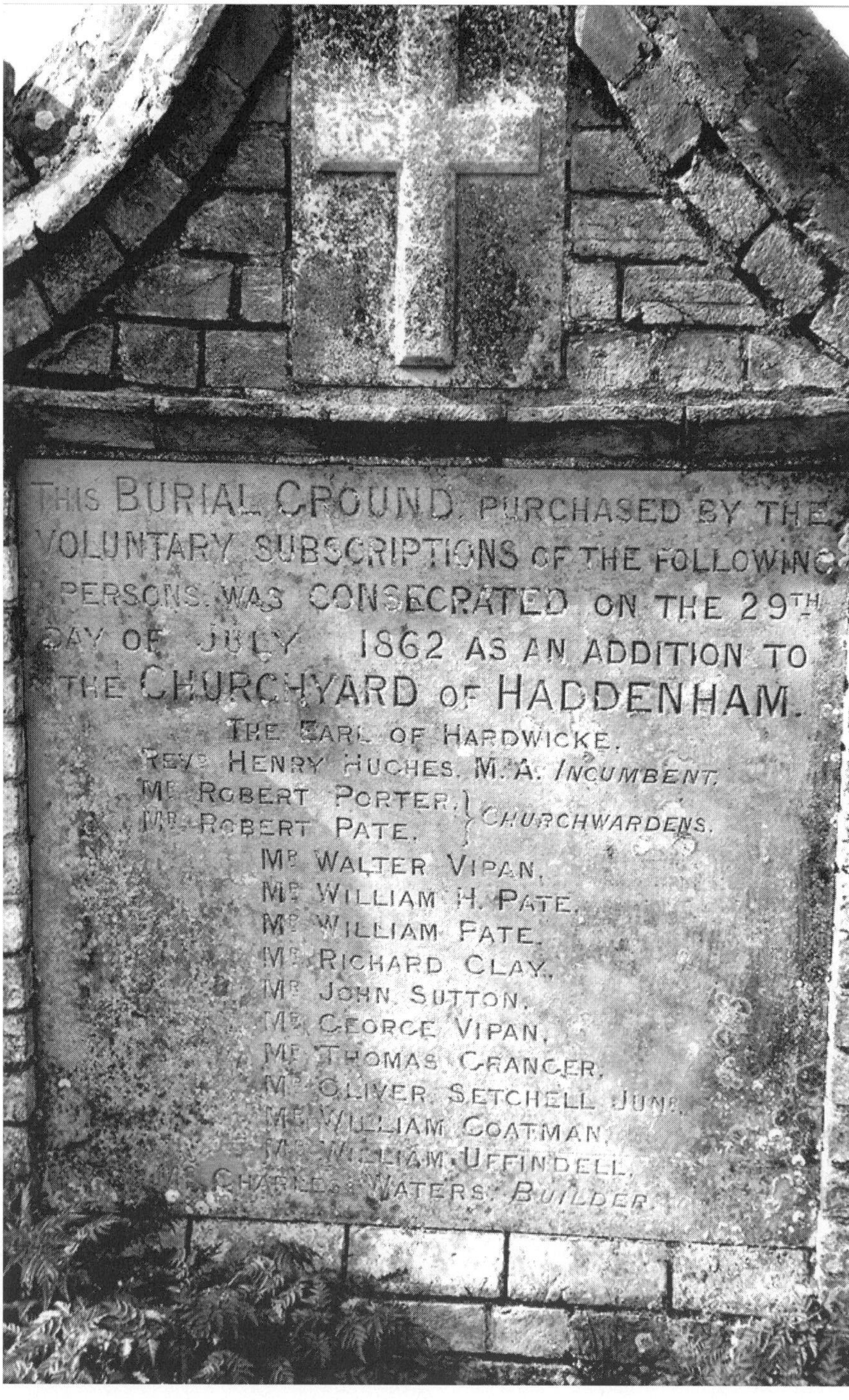

Stone plaque in the old burial ground in Church Lane now a wildlife garden. Note the well-known names: Revd Henry Hughes – who did so much for the village and is buried in this church yard – and the Porters, Pates, Suttons, and Vipans, all of which families have died out.

Top Corner: Mr Alfred Bethell's shoemaker's shop, and Sun Dial House, at the end of the 19th century. It was stipulated that when the house was pulled down in 1903 the sundial would be put back into the Baptist Chapel that replaced it. Note the ornate gas lamp on corner of what was The Windmill Public House (12). The child in the elegant push chair is supposedly George Adams, whose mother was landlady of The Vine (21) at the lower end of the High Street.

Hospital Sunday float (1927) beneath the sundial on the Baptist Chapel, whence it was transferred from Sun Dial House (*above*).

The Baptist Chapel at the time when the new meeting room was being added to its west end. The timber framed Three Kings Public House (11) is on the other side of the road. The foundation stone of the Baptist Chapel was laid on 22 November 1904. The spire was added later, in memory of William Chivers of Histon, one of whose farms was in Haddenham Parish, and who was a village benefactor.

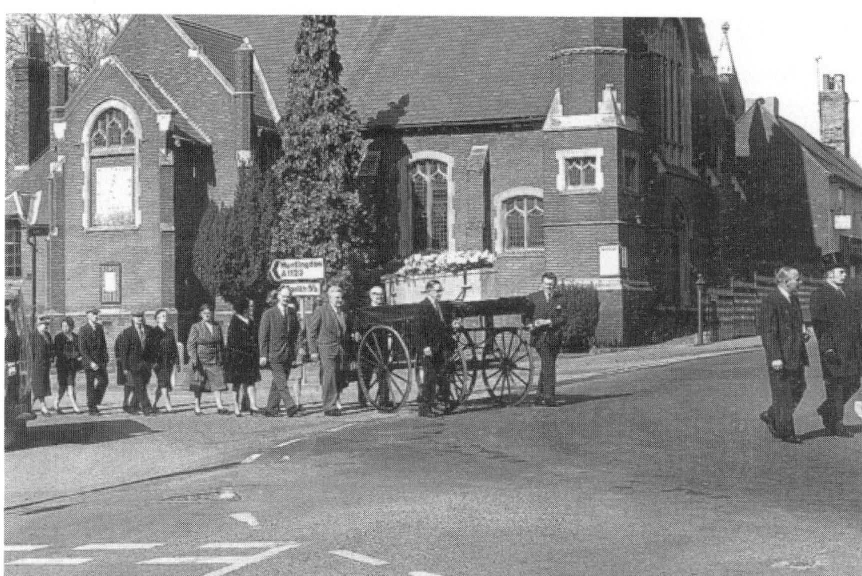

A funeral conducted in 1972 by village undertaker Alwyn Carter (extreme right, with Parish Clerk Charles Bester) was that of builder Sydney Feast who was a previous village undertaker. The hand-pulled bier was used by special request.

Looking down Station Road; the chemist's shop with its lamp, and children outside Newman's saddler's shop next door. The hill slopes down to the station, with The Red Lion public house (3) opposite the church and the gable end of AE Wright's stabling for his 'new' house The Lodge (later the Doctor's Surgery), just visible on the right.

There has been a pharmacy on these premises in Station Road for over a century – as we step back through the years, we record the names of Payne, Battersby, Davies, Blankley, Cottis, Green (who produced some excellent postcard views of Haddenham) and Langham.

Tom, Harry and William Newman; Mrs Newman and daughter Etheldreda (whose brother's name was Ovin) are looking from the window above.

Tom Newman's saddler's shop was in Station Road; the cottage is still there next to the Arkenstall Centre car park and lived in by Etheldreda's daughter. There was another saddler's shop, Longstaff's, along Hop Row in what is now part of The Three Kings car park.

Phil Hard the Blacksmith outside his shop which stood in what is now the Arkenstall Centre car park. There were at least three blacksmiths in the village; others were Walter Miller at 6 Aldreth Road, and at West End near the entrance to Hardwicke Fields. There is a broadshare made by Walter Miller in the Haddenham Bygones Collection at the School.

In the will of Robert Arkenstall dated 1640, provision was made for the establishment of a school for boys in Haddenham. Here the photo shows children of the present century in the school yard in 1964. This school dates from 1863, and replaced an earlier one on the same site.

From 1863, girls and infants (mixed) were taught in the school in High Street (recently converted to domestic use *see* page 38). The boys from 7 upwards were taught in the Robert Arkenstall School. From 1955 the boys' and girls' schools were amalgamated. The new school for 5–11 year olds was built in Camping Close in 1974.

A group of Robert Arkenstall boys with headmaster Arthur Miles, father of the later headmaster Bert Miles.

When the new Robert Arkenstall School was built in Camping Close, the old buildings were acquired by the Parish Council for conversion to a village centre. A small hall was added at the back, and a large hall with stage to the left of the old school buildings. The village library is housed in the old Headmaster's house on the right.The Arkenstall Centre is the focus for much of the social life of the village.

The Arkenstall Village Centre has staged a pantomime since 1971. The elaborate productions are now famed far and wide. This is a rescue scene from *Quest for a Princess* (1988).

Representatives of all village clubs and societies make up the Committee that runs the Arkenstall Village Centre. Every May, the Centre co-ordinates the village open day Blossoms and Bygones. The first was held in 1971 as a spring celebration of the Haddenham orchards (blossoms) and the Farmland Museum (bygones).

Holy Trinity Church stands a little way down the west side of Station Road. It is thought that there has been a church on this site since the time of St Etheldreda (630–679), who founded what is now Ely Cathedral.

The church in Haddenham was founded by Etheldreda's steward, Ovin, whose memorial stone stood at the road junction before it was moved to Ely Cathedral in 1770.

Holy Trinity once had a spire, shown in the picture above.

The Church was rebuilt in 1876 – but alas, with no spire. Funds collected for the work were taken by a certain villager to pay for his passage to America.

The church choir in 1904

Back row: A E Wright, Whetstone, –, –, –, Billy Mills, Revd Crookham, –, Arthur Miles, –, Revd Williams, –, –, –, –, –, Bert Miles, E L Porter.
Middle row: Ada Hawes, Mrs Ashby.
Front row: –, –, G Chapman, F Thulborn, Marsden Porter, –, Leonard Powers, George Bethell. The names of some of those in the front row are to be found on the War Memorial.

The Bishop of Ely, Rt Revd Stephen Sykes, with the Vicar, Revd Dr Michael Wadsworth, the churchwardens, the choir, and the members of the Roof Repair Fund committee at the launch of the Fund in 1994.

Sam Whetstone (left) clockwinder, Sydney Feast the builder and Richard (Dick) Sired on top of the tower of the Holy Trinity Church before the hole left for the spire-that-never-was was covered and safety railings installed in the 1960s.

Tree-lined Church Lane leading from West End to Station Road. Note the brick walls, a particular feature of Haddenham.

Laying the foundation stone of the Church Hall 29 October 1906. The Hall became a private dwelling in the mid-1970s.

The new Vicarage (*left*) was built in the late 1970s and the Old Vicarage became a private house, re-named Church End.

Vine House is further down Station Road, once the home of the Porters (yet another butchers). The red-brick building further down on left is York Villa, once the home of the Hepher family, renowned makers of Cambridgeshire Cheese which was regularly supplied to London by rail.

Looking down Station Road with the sign of The White Lion (2) hanging out over the street – now the headquarters of Barnes Transport. York Villa stands on the left, and the Burystead is in the distance.

Probably the most attractive approach to the villages – The Limes on the left, Madingley House, The Burystead, York Villa and the Maltings (now Vine House, formerly Porters the Butchers) on the right with the church tower dominating the skyline.

Northumbria Close off Station Road was built in the mid-90s. Its name reflects St Ethedreda's connections with that wild county.

The Pond – like the ones in Hillrow, Mill End and Froize End – has now been filled in. Ponds were once an important part of village life – for washing the feet of working horses and for soaking cart wheels in hot weather to tighten the spokes: remember Constable's much-loved picture *The Haywain*. This area was planted with willows to commemorate the Festival of Britain in 1951.

The old pond area in October 1999. In spring, it is filled with bulb flowers planted by the Friends of Haddenham.

Haddenham's northern boundary crosses farmland with North Fen to the west and Grunty Fen to the east. Leaving the village by the A1421 takes you across the old railway bridge and then, two miles further on, to the main A142.

Just beyond the old railway bridge to the left is the field in which the Haddenham Steam Rally is held every September. Evidence of ridge-and-furrow cultivation can be seen in the field car park.

Enthusiasts come to the Haddenham Steam Rally from all over the country, but retired Haddenham engineer Stan Burgess has less far to travel.

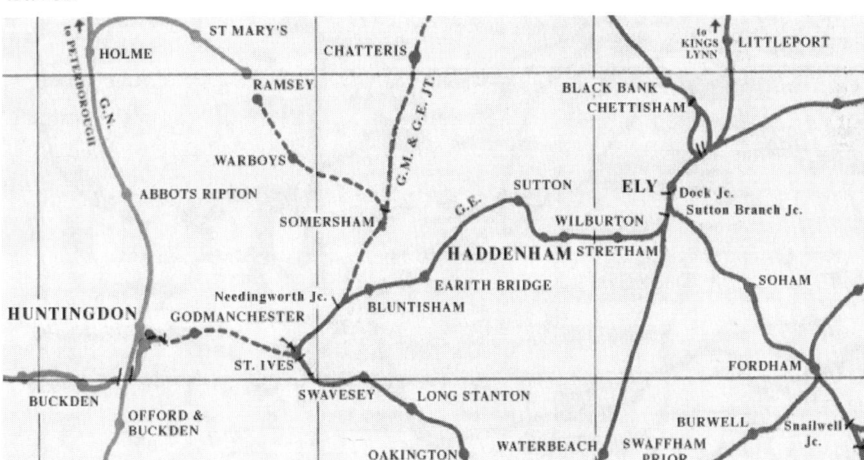

Until the 1920s, many villages were served by the railways, but the network began to decline as a result of the increased reliability and undoubted convenience of road transport. This map is dated 1923. Many people regret the 'axe' wielded by British Railways' Chairman Dr Beeching in the 1960s. but it was right for the times. Ely is still an important junction, but the line to St Ives is irrecoverable.

The route from Ely to Sutton was known as the Grunty Fen Express. Opened in 1864, it closed to passengers in 1932, though the line remained open for freight till 1960. As late as the 1950s, day excursions were run to Hunstanton.

The Station building became a Guide Camp and is now part of Anson Packaging (making plastic containers for such firms as Marks & Spencer)

Farm produce – milk, potatoes, sugarbeet and livestock – formed the bulk of the railway's business. In term time, school children for Soham Grammar and Ely High travelled by train.

Up to the First World War the weekly trip to Ely, Cambridge or St Ives was made by carrier's cart, bicycle or train. The coming of the Haddenham District Motor Service was a great boon; the service originated at Stretham; Parnell's Bus Company was in operation in the 1920s. Today, Haddenham has bus links with places as far away as King's Lynn, Peterborough and Wisbech, but most families have cars.

Haulage firms were established to carry farm and garden crops. Local loads were collected by Bethell, Green, Patterson and Salmons; Jack Richards started with one lorry in the late 1950s and the firm of Barnes & Son developed on Station Hill with Badcocks at Hillrow Causeway.

Milk was collected by Woolstenholmes – later to become the Milk Marketing Board – at Hillrow, and now the firm of Clarkes.

At one time there were three brick works in Haddenham, on both sides of the road near Station Bridge. One Frederick Jewson went on to national fame. All that is now left are ponds where the clay was excavated, and this photo of the brick workers. The man in the centre of the front row is Mr Cockle.

In the 1960s, the old brick pits belonged to the anthropologist Nicholas Guppy, after whose grandfather the tropical fish is named. As well as the brick workings, the site and buildings once housed the Haddenham Gasworks. When the land was sold, Guppy's Ponds were presented to the Parish Council, and are now maintained by a Pond Committeee as a wild-life sanctuary.

Chewell's Close is a private estate built in the early 1960s. It takes its name from the manor of Chewells – named after the 13th-Century Richard de Chewell.

At one time the home of Tom Ward, The Limes in Station Road is a building of the 18th Century on an earlier core, which has been extensively altered over the years. Much of its land has been sold off for development. It has a three-seater closet in the garden.

The general store in Station Road which belonged to Brooks and later Oxer. It stands on the hill next to The White Lion (2), now Barnes Transport.

View from Merrick Lane (off Station Road) across Guppy's ponds and the industrial park to Witchford on the ridge.

View from Merrick Lane across Grunty Fen to the aptly-named 'Ship of the Fens dominating the skyline.

View from the Cemetery across to the 'pepper-pot' tower of Sutton Church. This Parish graveyard replaced the Nonconformist ground (off The Green) and the Anglican one (in Church Lane) in the early 1920s.

Another view of the cemetery where members of all denominations – and of none – rest. Reqiuescant in Pace.

On the right hand side of Station Road opposite the end of Church Lane stands Merrick House. Jessie Tebbutt JP lived here; later it belonged to Jean Richards MBE, a retired director of the Citizens' Advice Bureaux, and founder of HEART (Haddenham Equipment and Resuscitation Trust) who was also for many years editor of the local magazine *Village Voice*.

Looking up Station Road towards Top Corner – left foreground is The Three Kings (11), then a butcher's shop, then The Windmill (12) – later Mr Steel's bicycle shop. Across the crossroads is Tebbutt's corner shop. Note the prominent gas lamp on the chemist's shop (*right*).

The Three Kings (*left*), is an old coaching inn with a priest's hole and even a secret underground passage running to the church – or so the story goes. The entrance on the left was for the coaches whose exit was in Hop Row. The coach entrance was blocked up in the 1960s and restored in 1999 when Greene King refurbished the premises – re-opened on 14 December. The house to the right was for many years a butcher's, one of at least four in Haddenham in the 1980s.

The old Windmill (12) Public House, that became the bicycle shop run by Mr 'Chemmy' Steel until he moved down to Victors at 17 High Street into the building that replaced Palmer's the pork butcher.

Windmill Corner today: Station Road to the left, Hop Row to the right. When the traffic became heavier in the 1930s, Mr Steel moved his cycle shop down to Victors so that the building could be demolished to afford drivers a better view at the corner.

Hop Row, the eastern arm of the A1123 to Wilburton, Stretham, Wicken and Soham.

Steel's Bakery from the 1950s has now been divided into shops.

The car park of The Three Kings in Hop Row, the site of a Saxon burial ground.

Saxon graves were discovered when the car park of The Three Kings was excavated in 1990. A man in his fifties and a woman in her late teens lay together, he with a spear, knife, shield boss and iron buckle; she with amber, glass and silver beads, a bone brooch and tweezers, and a bone spindle whorl. The bones and artefacts were taken away for further investigation and treatment.

Paddock Way – so called because the land was once Farmer AE Wright's paddock.

Robin Maclaren owned the last garage and filling station in Haddenham, demolished to make way for Hinton View. Before this, it was the headquarters of Burkitts, engineers and steam tackle owners.

Hinton View. AC Benson, Master of Magdalene from 1904, rented Hinton Hall as his country escape from Cambridge. A son of the Archbishop of Canterbury, he wrote the words for England's second national anthem – *Land of Hope and Glory* – perhaps at Hinton Hall. Less than a century ago, he was to be seen with manservant and other retainers walking from the Hall, and along Merrick Lane, for morning service at Holy Trinity.

The approach to Haddenham from the east – the Water Tower and communications mast are visible for miles. The first tower was built in the late 1920s (when piped water came to the village); the present one replaced it in 1962. Anglia Water occasionally allows visitors to climb to the top to take in the fantastic views.

Enthusiastic archaeologists suggest that the Mound on the Recreation Ground is nothing more than a look-out point or feature in the garden of the Seventeenth-century Hinton Hall, whose ruins were excavated by Leeds University in 1970.

The Ramparts on the east side of the Recreation Ground; here is the 'Home Industrial built by F Peacock & Son 1921' – a pair of substantial semis for the family.

A view across the Recreation Ground to the west, showing both the spire of the Baptist Church and the tower of Holy Trinity.

The pavilion on the Recreation Ground was rebuilt in the 1990s. As the twentieth century draws to a close, a skateboard area is under construction.

The Bier House, Hop Row, once the home of the Parish bier. This part of Parish history was unfortunately disposed of some years ago . . .

. . . but has been tracked down for a photo-call.

'Pakey' – George Pake – moves part of the Haddenham Gasworks (which was down by the station), via the High Street, to Lode Way.

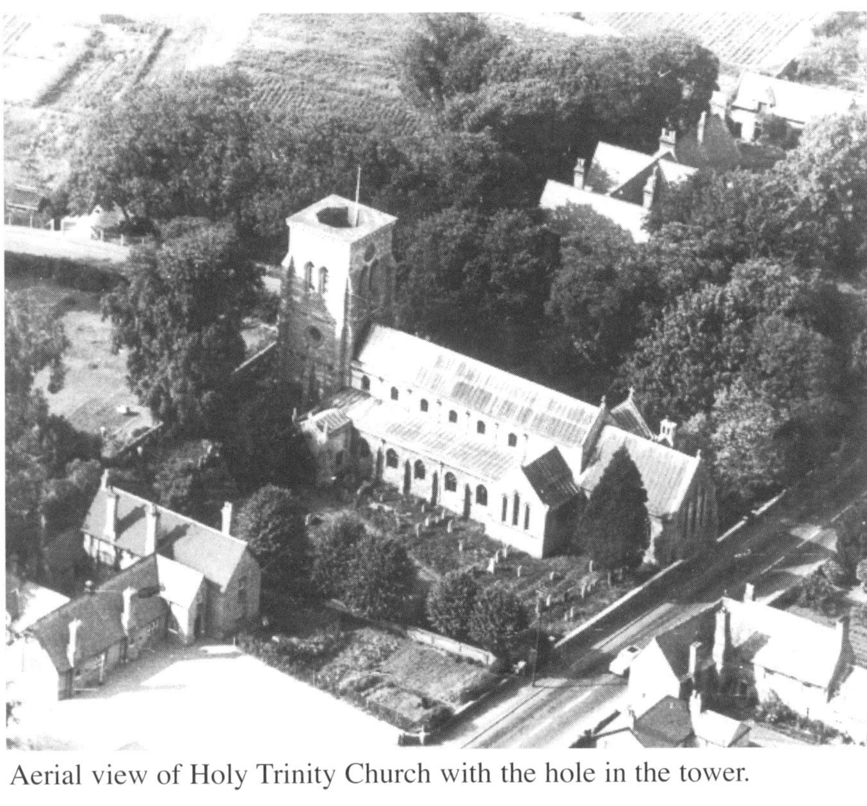

Aerial view of Holy Trinity Church with the hole in the tower.

In 1914 the Parish Council bought land for the Recreation Ground from the Hardwicke Estate. A wide range of sporting facilities is now available for the general public including floodlit courts and an excellent play area for the young generation.

Photo by H.E. Langham (chemist)

Hardwicke Cricket Eleven 1895

EL Porter, RM Croft, O Ryland (capt), Walt Hawes, A Palmer, JJ Neville, T Newman (scorer), A Gateson, G Gosden, William Hawes, J Gateson (umpire), RG Uffindel, M Hovell.

The Young Farmers' Club was one of earliest in the Isle. This YFC Hockey Team played in the 1950s.

Haddenham has always been enthusiastic over its football especially in the early days when all members of the teams lived in the village.

Haddenham Rovers 2nd XI

Cambs Division Champions

Standing: John Bethell, Jack Hawes, Andy Ashfield, Robert Norman, Andy Spragg, Tony Morton

Seated: Tizer Easy, Leon Doggett, Malcolm Sadler, Jim Yarrow, Ken Morton

Music has played a big part in village life over the years – the Haddenham Silver Band was established in 1894, and is still going today. There are now Church and WI Choirs, the Haddenham Singers and hand-bell teams, and concerts are often given in one of the churches, or the Arkenstall Village Centre.

The Haddenham Silver Band in late Victorian times

Boys' Brigade Bugle Band 1905

The Haddenham Silver Band in the late 1990s.

Blossoms & Bygones: Haddenham Singers at Church End (1990s)
directed alfresco by Mrs Elizabeth Stead

Costume chorus – Spring Concert 1991

Reception – Miss K Shelton
Back row: Chloe Flack, Angus Gannage-Stewart, Rachel Manning, Jessica Wright, Amy Allen, Nathan Brown, Josie Shipp, Jessica Mynott
Middle row: Sophie Housden, Stephanie Marshall, Stephanie Bowles, Nicole Cruse, Ami Craven, Bukami Cameron, Alan Wilding, Paige Collins, Molly Blacknell
Front row: Matthew Wenn, Jamie Chapman, Dee Rutterford, Coral Spicer, Callum Brown, Oliver Dennis, Jonathan Cook, Emma Lowe.
Absent: Catherine Brown, Thomas Holden, Kayley Norman

Reception – Mrs Hunns, Mrs Burgess (Nursery Nurse)
Back row: Adam Johnson, Benedict Squires, Timothy Lucraft, Lewis Bendall-Craft, Thomas Bottomley, Sam Lapthorn, Bethany Carey
Middle row: Jessica Lenton, Harry Bristow, Jamie Woor, Rebecca Williams, Rosie Peck, Poppy Skipp, Thomas Redford, Meghan Wilson, Bridgette Wilson
Front row: Bethany Spalding, Megan Holland, Matthew Burrows, Michael Thomas, Shane Barber, Chloe Barton, Ben Cogan, Charlie Linsey, Daniel Coulson
Absent: Ryan Norman

Year 1 – Mrs Young (Supply Teacher)
Back row: Ben Hughes, Callum Welsh, Charlie Sawyer, Rebecca Emmerson, Tayla Sawyer, Charlotte Spry, Grace Kemp, Tanya Piggott
Middle row: Georgia Arnold, Sian McGrath, Amanda Hamstra, Andre Henriques, Mark Rogers, Annie Ryan, Holly Hibbert, Victoria Chamberlain, Eleanor Ideson
Front row: Christle McLachlan, Alex Minall, Daniel Norman, Alex Snooks, Jamie Coulson, Poppy Bendall-Craft, Erica Jamieson, Laura Bevis, Elysia Good
Absent: Mrs Redhead (Full-time Teacher), William Dixon, Ben Poulter

Year 2 – Mrs S Richards (General Assistant) Mrs A Wildman (Teacher)
Back row: Oliver King, Zoë Emery, Shonnie Spicer, Stephanie Roberts, Thomas Edwards, Joseph Badhams, Oliver Riches, Christopher Doak, Paul Dewey, Zackery Harmeyer
Middle row: Katie Tindall, Emily Norman, Kirstie Strangward, Helen Emery, Billie Newell, Jake Rutterford, Ben Stephen, Adam Clow, Corbie Barnard, Chantelle Todd, Eppie Le Roux
Front row: Teresa Andrus, Philip Murray, Jasmine Griffiths, Katherine Warburton, Stefan Le Roux, Carys Breeze, Thomas King, Megan Barnes, Amy Dive

Year 3 – Mr Sutton (Headteacher) Miss Berry (Teacher)
Back row: Kelly Gosling, Amy Johnson, Caitlin Breeze, Daniel Loades, Thomas Stell, Nate Wilson, Alex Jones, Austin Brown, Lawrence Spry, Pippa Howard
Middle row: David Niskin, Sam Barber, Matthew Ball, Mark Coles, Aidan Arnold, Amy Taylor, Emma Craven, Lily Mei-Li Dobson, James Butter, Sophie Minall
Front row: Christopher Thomas, Lewis Timbrell, Alice Newnum, Lily Kemp, Joshua Baker, Ben Manning, Jonathon Emerson, Matthew McGinty

Year 4 – Mrs Wilkerson (Assistant) Mr Schumm (Teacher)
Back row: Charlotte Mclachlan, Luke Chapman, Simon King, Scott Rogers, Joshua Todd, Adam Nimmo, Natasha Smith, Sophie Spriggs, Jasmine Pattern, Samantha Haslop, Becci Carnes, Daniel Redford, Samantha Chamberlin
Middle row: Kayleigh McGinty, Gina Kemp, Thomas Padmore, Huw Corcoran, Matthew Lucraft, Charles Howard Jones, Catherine Ideson, Emily Burgess, Hayley Coulson,Aaron Andras, Oliver Bond
Front row: Carly Munns, Alex Pedley, Daniel Riches, Philip Rossiter, Kayleigh Dewey, Pennie Keating, Louise Housden, Lexis Henrique, Hevlin Salter, Rebecca Norman
Absent: Kieran Granger, Daniel Peachey, Kirsty Smith

Year 5 – Karen Frazer (Teacher)
Back row: Chantelle Papworth, Andrew Wilding, Aaron Arnold, Ross Butter, Daniel McGrath, Anna Jones, Lucy Tindall, Samantha Bowles, Allana Money
Third row: Rebecca Barlow, Millie Newnum, Lucy Collier, Elizabeth Fletcher, Jacob Le Roux, Emma Newman, Claire Taylor, Becky Taberner, Coral Robinson
Second row: Rachael Gatehouse, Craig Timbrell, Daniel Taylor, James Loades, Adam Denniss, Billy Young, Nicholas MacCaulliffe, Sam Baker
Front row: Zoë Stell, Aimee Bond, Kate Bethell, Ben Nightingale, Imogen Mynott, Natalie King, Clare Brown, Jamie Howard
Absent: Scott Cheetham, Chris Holden, Chris Thoday

School Secretary:
Lynn Smith

Cooks:
Pat Last, Ruby Hook, Sharon Housden

Year 6 – Mrs Main (Supply Teacher)
Back row: Joe Blacknell, Melissa King, Philippa Barlow, William Padmore, Jake Gimpaolo, Hannah Housden, Phil Harle, Helen Gathercole, Adam Webdell
Middle row: Lee Diamond, Oliver Lucraft, Sam Barltrop, Daniel Haslop, Daryl Andrus, Edward Clark, Tom Moden, Charlotte Roberts
Front row: Lloyd Savage, Chris Wilkerson, Charlie Kemp, David Rose, Lizzie Francis, Melissa Bogunovic, Abbie Keating
Absent: Mrs Harford (Full-time Teacher), Emily Handley, Scott Williams

Dinner Ladies:
Back row: Betty Turner, Michelle Munns, Elaine Taylor, Jennifer Daly
Front row: Helen Money, Alison Wilkerson, Anne Roger

Haddenham Parish Council, November 1999
Back row: Peter Goddard, machinery partsman; Steve Edwards, postmaster; Jezz Davies, telecommunications consultant; Nick Tindall, bank manager; Stuart Smith (vice-chairman), data collector; Robert Norman, fruit grower; Rodney Dale, author and publisher; David Fairchild, farmer
Front row: George Gutkaess, retired council worker; Lyn Carter, jeweller; Ken Bowcock (chairman), semi-retired manager; Jenny Manning (clerk), housewife and mother; Sheila Searle, chief nursing officer (retired); Owen Bethell, retired nurseryman

Trustees of the Haddenham Charities, November 1999
Back row: Ken Bowcock, semi-retired manager; Ray Scott, fertilizer trader; Mervyn Salmons, garage owner; Robert Norman, fruit grower; Stuart Findlay, local family doctor; Colin Bidwell, farmer; David Fairchild, farmer
Front row: Ivor Wright, builder; Ven Jeff Watson, Archdeacon of Ely; Pam Turner, retired teacher; Pat Traylen, social worker; Shirley Pollard (Clerk to the Charities), chartered surveyor; John Last, seed handling and demonstration officer, National Institute of Agricultural Botany; Peter Handley, chrysanthemum grower
Absent: Trevor Carter, university computer officer

Trustees of the Robert Arkenstall Educational Foundation, November 1999
Back row: Ven Jeff Watson, Archdeacon of Ely; Robert Norman, fruit grower; Ivor Wright, builder; Dr Stuart Findlay, local family doctor; Cllr Philip Read, farmer; David Fairchild, farmer
Front row: Pam Turner, retired teacher; Ken Bowcock, semi-retired manager; John Last, seed handling and demonstration manager, NIAB; Shirley Pollard (Clerk to the Foundation), chartered surveyor; Jean Bowcock, nursery nurse; Peter Handley, chrysanthemum grower

The Haddenham Charities

were formed in 1980 from The Poors' Land Trust, The Charity of Sir John Jolles, The Grunty Fen Allotments and The Poors' Land Education Foundation. The Charity owns about 91 acres of land and formerly owned the site of the old High Street School. 1998 income was £7,335 from rents and £5,986 from investments.

The income is applied:
- to promote the education (including physical and social training) of people under the age of 25 years resident in the Parish,
- to relieve conditions of need, hardship or distress,
- for any charitable purposes for the general benefit of the inhabitants of the Parish.

The Robert Arkenstall Educational Foundation

was established by the will of Robert Arkenstall dated 1 April 1640, wherein about 50 acres of land were left to the Parish, the rents to be used to maintain a free school. (The school building became the Arkenstall Centre in 1972.) 1998 income was £2,285 from rents and £955 from investments.

One quarter of the net income is paid to the Vicar of Haddenham for the promotion of religious instruction by means of, for example, a Sunday School. The balance may be used for special benefits for the local school and for providing financial assistance to young persons under the age of 25 who are entering further education or training for a trade or profession.

The Haddenham Year

January is pantomime time: for the past 30 years an annual event which draws praise from all over the Eastern Region – it gives many local youngsters the chance to appear on stage, or to take part behind the scenes, and gives them confidence.
February St Valentine: for many years dinner dances were held to commemorate this date in what is often a very dull month.
March sees each of the churches celebrating Mothering Sunday (depending when Easter falls).
April brings Easter Celebrations with the churches often 'doing' Easter breakfasts as well as providing eggs for the children. There is often a Spring Concert or a musical evening towards the end of the month.
Since 1971, **May** is the month for the annual village open day – Blossoms & Bygones – which raises funds for the Arkenstall Centre and brings families together for the afternoon – just as the village Feasts used to before the war.
June sees the start of fêtes, barbecues and fairs for a variety of good causes, followed in **July** by the Friends of Haddenham Fen Ride on tractors and trailers – a MUST for all newcomers – with a picnic tea on the very top of North Hill. The last weekend of the month sees Arts & Flowers, the display of paintings and flower arrangements in Holy Trinity Church – another fund raiser for the Parish church.
September is the month to celebrate harvest in church and chapel, school and club. The YFC show, still going strong after 50 years, takes place in the Arkenstall Centre – a far cry from its inception in the mid-forties at College Farm. The Haddenham Steam Rally, in the second weekend, has become of national importance.
October brings the darker nights and Hallowe'en is celebrated by the uniformed organisations, followed closely in **November** by the Annual Fireworks Party and barbecue at Chewells Lane: the second Saturday is the date for the Ploughing Match at Hermitage Farm where teams both equine and mechanical compete from all over the country.
December brings the ever-popular carolling: for many years substantial funds have been raised for Tower Hospital and more recently the Princess of Wales Hospital in Ely in this seasonal way.

A review of life in Haddenham over the past 100 years

'Within living memory'

At the turn of the century, life in a Fen village was dominated by farming and its allied trades: there were blacksmiths, saddlers and horse doctors to take good care of that essential part of the workforce on the farms – the horse. There was even a bone and manure works which could make use of the dead carcasses.

The manpower needed for the farms lived in tied cottages and it was a feature each October to find out which families had moved into Chivers or Hinton homes: today the number of men employed on farms is minimal, and huge machines do the work of many men – not to mention the horses.

The Chivers estate at Aldreth was sold in the early sixties, as was the Hinton farm: today Agriserves owns Staple Leys and College Farm land, as well as a lot of the Hinton estate. The days of the smallholder, once a very common member of the village community, are over: it is no longer possible to get a living from 'two cows and a horse' with a pig kept solely 'for the pot'.

In her *Recollections of a Country Woman* Mabel Demaine recalls Goodening Day, when widows called at the larger houses on 21 December, St Thomas's Day, to ask for a little something for Christmas, usually a packet of tea or a little money: this, like Plough Monday when it was the turn of young men (often farm workers with no work) to collect alms from householders on a Monday in early January, died out in the twenties. Mayladying, for the girls to canvass help in the form of money (as little as a farthing) continued until after the second world war, although calling round at houses on St Valentine's Day in February was not as popular in Haddenham as in some other Cambridgeshire villages – Stretham, for example.

In 1904 there were 24 licensed public houses in the parish and now there are two – the Three Kings (known to have been an inn in 1727 when the first meeting of the Haddenham Drainage Commissioners took place there) and the Cherry Tree: the role played by these pubs was also as a Club for 'share outs' pre NHS days. Drunkenness was part of the village scene as late as the fifties, particularly fighting on The Green.

The brickworks offered employment for a considerable number of men up to 1932: evidence of locally-produced bricks and tiles can be spotted in local buildings and a large collection of bricks from all over the country can be viewed at the privately-owned Brick & Tile Museum in Hillrow.

Buildings that have 'come and gone' this century include the Mission Hall in Hillrow, the Baptist Chapel in Aldreth, the Farmland Museum (from 1969 to 1992 very much part of the High Street scene), the corn businesses of Healey Wilson in High Street and Setchells on the Green, the Milk Marketing Depot (once the firm of Woolstenholmes and the site now occupied by Clarks Hauliers), the HQ for Richards Transport, now a housing estate (Lester Drive), and the English Provender Factory (makers of such delights as Gentleman's Relish) has moved away; local dairies (Palmers & Wards) closed long ago. Activity at the old station has expanded to provide hundreds of jobs manufacturing plastic trays and cartons for such firms as Marks & Spencer. Farm barns have been converted to residential use (*eg* the cheese factory at York Villa and barns in Hillrow) and the two halls built for church use in 1906 are now family homes.

What is new? Haddenham now has a modern doctors' surgery on the site of the old Baptist Chapel on The Green: the Recreation Field boasts a modern sports centre with fine facilities, and the old school buildings have been replaced with modern facilities at Camping Close. The Village Centre (named after Robert Arkenstall), opened in 1972 is one of the finest in the district, and a Social Club with its own licensed bar is situated in Chewells Lane adjacent to the Playgroup which has its foundations way back in the early sixties in the Vicarage. Modern private housing estates now occupy what, at the turn of the century, was orchard land, and old people are catered for in Camping Close, a sheltered housing complex off the High Street. Council-built houses at Cherry Orchard, Perry Close, Newtown and Station Road are fast becoming privately-owned and a mobile home park is provided on a field once owned by the Lord of the Manor, Earl Harwicke (Wimpole Hall in the south of the county was the family seat – now National Trust property).

The biggest event for 'locals' is obviously the floods of 1947 about which much has been written: there were less-severe floods in 1937. The two world wars took their toll of young lives as can be seen from the list of names on the Memorial on The Green. Two archaeological digs in Hillrow Fen hit the national press, and the discovery of a Quaker Burial Ground in Mill End and a Saxon Burial Site in the Three Kings Car Park also spread the fame of the village.

Books have been written, photos taken, videos made and even a web site has been put on the internet just for Haddenham so, although as one newspaper stated 'Haddenham is the wrong side of Cambridge', it does not seem to have done too badly over the past 100 years.

Lorna Delanoy